George Frideric Handel

MESSIAH

IN FULL SCORE

Edited by ALFRED MANN

DOVER PUBLICATIONS, INC.・New York

Published in Canada by General Publishing Company, Ltd.,
30 Lesmill Road, Don Mills, Toronto, Ontario.
Published in the United Kingdom by Constable and Company, Ltd.

This Dover edition, first published in 1989, is an unabridged
republication of *Messiah: An Oratorio,* Parts I, II, and III, originally
published by Rutgers University Documents of Music in 1961, 1959,
and 1965, respectively. The work is published by special arrangement
with Joseph Boonin and Jerona Music Corporation.

Available in the music trade through Jerona Music Corporation
P.O. Box 5010, S. Hackensack, N.J. 07606
Complete orchestral parts also available through Jerona Music Corporation

Manufactured in the United States of America
Dover Publications, Inc.
31 East 2nd Street
Mineola, N.Y. 11501

Library of Congress Cataloging-in-Publication Data

Handel, George Frideric, 1685-1759.
Messiah.

Oratorio.
English words.
Libretto by Charles Jennens, taken from the Bible and
Prayer book Psalter.
Reprint. Originally published: New Brunswick, N.J.:
Rutgers, the State University, 1959-65.
(Rutgers University documents of music ; no. 6).
Includes critical commentary.
1. Oratorios—Scores. 2. Jesus Christ—Songs and Music.
I. Mann, Alfred, 1917-   . II. Jennens, Charles, 1700-1773. lbt.   III. Title.
M2000.H22M298 1989   89-752494
ISBN 0-486-26067-4

CONTENTS

PART II

PART III

INTRODUCTION
Sources and Performance

Handel's *Messiah* holds an extraordinary place both among the composer's works and in the history of Western music — no other work has met with the same wide and enduring response. Thus it also holds an extraordinary place in the history of performance: it is the only work of its time that has seen a continuous sequence of revivals, for almost two decades under the direction of the composer, for two further decades under conductors who had shared Handel's work on the London scene, and for the two following centuries through the devotion of generation after generation.

In the course of this long performance history, the wish to adhere closely to the composer's own practice was followed by gestures of conscious departure and eventually by efforts of conscientious return. The most widespread departure was prompted not so much by stylistic orientation as by conditions of society. The work became, especially in the English speaking world, the property of nearly every choral organization, and the principal demand for *Messiah* performances arose in situations in which the participation of an orchestra seemed out of the question. Meanwhile the music publishing trade had created a concept essentially foreign to Handel's time — the piano-vocal score whose use for gratis performance by choirs of any desired size, while the accompaniment was reduced to a single instrument, provided a welcome solution to the problem of economy. What this solution ignored was not only the gross distortion of the Handelian score but, curiously, also how closely the composer's intentions were missed. In the composition of *Messiah* Handel himself was guided by an unusual wish for economy. Not certain what instrumental forces he would find in Dublin, for whose charitable institutions the work was first presented, and having to plan for a performance off home base, Handel had designed the majority of arias for obbligato accompaniment by a single instrumental part (in which first and second violins joined); thus the addition of one instrument would help the present-day choirmaster in these cases to take the crucial step of restoring the keyboard part to its continuo function and to regain the qualities of timbre and balance intended.

The entire orchestration is unusually modest; the plain string texture of the overture dominates the autograph score, additional parts for trumpets and kettledrums appearing most sparingly. There are no instrumental solos except for one: the trumpet part in the Last Judgment scene. Oboe and bassoon parts are not contained in Handel's autograph score; serving merely in a doubling function, these parts were added later to Handel's performance material (obbligato oboe parts are found in one exceptional instance, apparently inspired by the text "Their sound is gone out", in Chorus No. 39, which was also added later to the original score). Horns were probably used at times as a tutti doubling for the trumpets — two horn players are listed in the budgets for Handel's *Messiah* performances in London — but in this case no separate parts seem to have been written out.[1] There are also no extant parts for double bass, though the use of the instrument is implied by the distinction between *Violonc.* and *tutti* in Handel's autograph score. These indications coincide with changes from bass clef to tenor clef and vice versa — their alternate use in the cello part may thus be understood in the sense of *senza basso* and *col basso*. The budgets for Handel's performances show payments for two double bass players, one evidently reading from the stand for the solo cello and the other from the stand of the two tutti cellos.[2] In his earliest performances of the work, Handel seems to have employed a very small string group. At a later point he added notations for a ripieno-concertino division of an apparently enlarged orchestra (*con rip.* and *senza rip.*). According to one of the preserved budgets, four of a total of twelve violinists and one double bass player received a higher pay scale in compensation for solo responsibilities involved — primarily the accompaniment of the arias, but also of certain chorus portions (especially those in which a change of tempo calls for a more responsive manner of accompaniment).

The wish to render both the economy of Handel's scoring and its subtle differentiations was the prime factor leading to the extended plan of issuing a new *Messiah* edition. The first volume of the score appeared in the Handel anniversary year 1959, and the publication of instrumental parts was undertaken in anticipation of the Handel anniversary in 1985. It was the editor's good fortune that this span of time was marked by decisive advances in Handel research. The project of publishing the three volumes of the score coincided in time with Watkins Shaw's work in issuing a modern *Messiah* edition for Novello, accompanied by a highly informative critical commentary, and with the appearance of Jens Peter Larsen's pathbreaking study concerned with the origins, composition, and sources of the work. The same period saw the rise of general awareness of the argument of authenticity in modern interpretation. Though a contradiction in terms — no interpreter can deny his identity — the "authentic approach" justifiably has become a contemporary ideal in *Messiah* performance. While our attempts to present a faithful text for the score and orchestral parts of the work are obviously dedicated to this ideal, they must be accompanied by a word of caution: "The purely historical performance is only a phantom created by polemic imagination."[3] Since we cannot remove the differences of time and conditions and since the study of the original performance situation is bound to be a continuing effort, we cannot escape the mandate of ever new responsibility in taking issue with the model of *Messiah* presentations that began on April 13, 1742.

When Handel went to Dublin, he took with him two scores of the work and a set of vocal and instrumental parts. The scores were his autograph, which he had written two months earlier in the span of twenty-four days, and a fair copy made by his amanuensis John Christopher Smith. The latter copy served as Handel's conducting score, and he kept it in use for eighteen years — the last *Messiah* performance he directed took place nine days before his death. In the course of time, Handel made numerous changes in the work, most of which are reflected in the conducting score but — with very few exceptions — not in the autograph. The conducting score also served as a basis for the parts, as is evident from minor copying errors that were taken over into these.

Handel's immediate concern was to check the accuracy of the vocal parts. Detained by unfavorable weather in the town of Chester, he enlisted the help of the Cathedral organist in arranging a reading session with local singers, and an anecdote recorded by the historian Charles Burney relates that the composer flew into a rage at the efforts of one of them who, as he said, could sing at sight "but not at first sight". The original performance parts, probably written by Smith with the assistance of other copyists, are lost; but according to a codicil in Handel's will, a new set of parts was presented, with a new score, to the London Foundling Hospital for which Handel gave yearly benefit performances. They were received within two months of Handel's death and have been preserved in the Foundling Hospital's archives. The autograph score is in the British Library. Handel's conducting score, which formed part of the collection of St. Michael's College, Tenbury, at the time this edition was begun, is now in the Bodleian Library, Oxford. The variants and interdependence of these manuscripts, and the performance history they describe, are discussed in the Critical Notes.

In offering a new edition based on the sources, the principal aim has been to render their original appearance in a manner that is practicable and immediately understandable. With the wondrous wealth the sources contain, there is a sparseness in their appearance that is most instructive for the modern performer. Handel usually omitted the notation of parts that represented a doubling, so that the actual polyphonic texture is directly apparent in the score. Similarly, in writing out the parts, Handel's copyists omitted any indications that could easily be supplied by the context; but they added some which must have emanated from the rehearsal situation. Thus there is no complete consistency in the sources for the performance material — such consistency was apparently not considered mandatory in an age in which the creative process was so closely linked to performance. Conversely, while the instrumental parts contain no cues other than occasional reference to the end of the preceding verbal text they invariably include the fully written out vocal part for the sensitive ensemble task of the accompanied recitatives. Details of score and parts have been collated in the edition as far as possible. Roman type has been used to present primary source notations, Italic type has been used for notations merely implied through secondary sources, and editorial additions have been placed in parentheses.

In view of the advances of modern Handel research and the insight into Handelian performance practice it has afforded the modern interpreter, it is remarkable that the performance of the vocal parts, both for soloists and chorus, remains the most formidable challenge. To begin with, there are no original indications for differences in dynamics: the singers of Handel's time were guided in their interpretation solely by the verbal text. Nor was there a complete distinction between soloists and choristers; as the set of Foundling Hospital parts shows, the soloists sang also in the chorus. Some of the soloists were, in fact, drawn from the chorus in the first place, and their number varied; but there were usually more than four. As the records for Handel's performances show, he had in mind three different types of alto soloists. Aside from the famous Mrs. Cibber, two countertenors served as soloists in the Dublin performances; the arias No. 6 and No. 36, originally intended for bass, were re-written, after various interim revisions, for a castrato. The solo appearance of the principal soprano was often saved for the aria "Rejoice", the solos in the Nativity scene being sung by a secondary soloist, in some of Handel's performances by a boy. Boys sang the choral soprano part, countertenors the choral alto part; but since the soloists participated in the chorus, the sound of both sections was marked by an intriguing mixture, enhanced, in the soprano section, by the supporting oboe parts.

In some measure, the varying assignments of vocal solo parts give an account of the problems Handel encountered in rehearsals for the first *Messiah* performance. The principal soprano and alto soloists had come with him from London, the former being an Italian *prima donna* not familiar with English traditions, and the latter an English actress not trained in the *bel canto* style — both, however, accomplished artists. The tenor, bass, and countertenor soloists were members of the Dublin Cathedral choirs. Apparently, Handel had overestimated their qualifications and was consequently obliged to make drastic adjustments in their roles. Here begins the complex story of changing versions for individual numbers of the work, a story doubly arresting because the composer retained some of the revisions for later performances in London where soloists of his choice were available: he did so apparently for purely artistic reasons. Larsen has traced the entire history of original *Messiah* performances that thus unfolded, claiming in the end that the formulation of a "definitive" *Messiah* version cannot be fully attained. In the present edition an attempt has been made to draw the consequences from Larsen's findings and approach Handel's final or preferred choices for a complete form of the work; thus alternate versions are described in the Critical Notes but are not given in the musical text.

The account of Handel's vocal forces and its implications for the form of the work point out to the modern singer concerned with the question of baroque ornamentation that the original application of this dramatic practice greatly varied. In Handel's earliest *Messiah* performances only one Italian opera soloist was in his cast: the principal soprano — and who would dare add further embellishments to the aria "Rejoice"! With the general change from Italian to English singers, which accompanied the turn from opera to oratorio in Handel's work, improvised ornamentation lost its importance, and the use of the da capo form — foremost arena for vocal improvisation — began to decline. Thus the edition contains next to no suggested embellishments; with minor exceptions, none were apparently intended.[4]

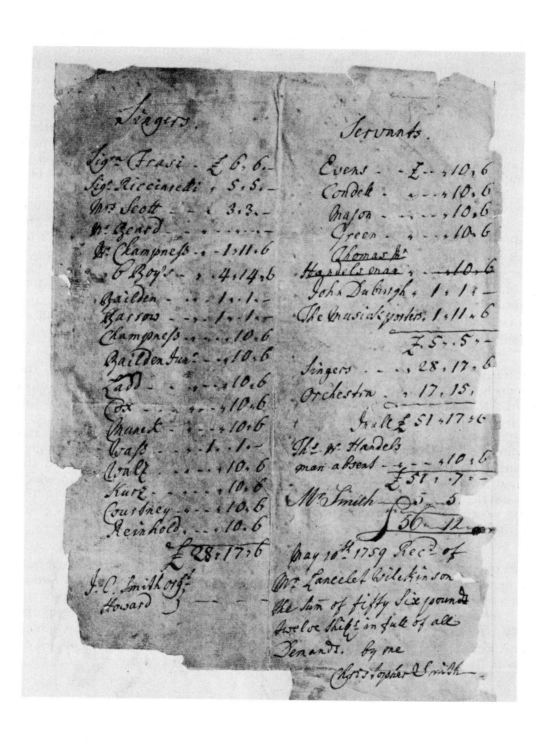

General Bill for the *Messiah* performance at the Foundling Hospital on May 3, 1759
Reproduced by permission of the Thomas Coram Foundation, London

Improvisation played a decisive role, however, in the execution of the keyboard continuo performed by the composer himself. Handel conducted his performances from the harpsichord; an organ accompaniment was left to the assistant conductor charged with the training of the choir and consisted apparently of no more than a discreet doubling of choral texture wherever the rehearsal experience had indicated the advisability of such support. The keyboard part in this edition, therefore, is by necessity merely an outline suggestion. The relative importance of harpsichord and organ accompaniment is illustrated by the document that marked the historic step from Handel's own to subsequent performances of the work (see the facsimile reproduction). The Foundling Hospital performance in 1759 was scheduled for May 3rd, and the extant expense accounts, preserved in the Foundling Hospital archives, laconically record the changes in preparation that took place after April 14, the day of Handel's death. The name of Thomas Bramwall, Handel's servant, who guided the blind composer to the harpsichord, was crossed out, and his fee was deducted from the total with the note: "Th⁵ Mr. Handel's man absent". The assistant conductor, son of John Christopher Smith who had been Handel's student, was replaced by another organist, Samuel Howard, and took the conductor's chair at the harpsichord. The responsibility for *Messiah* performances had passed to posterity.

Grateful acknowledgment is made to my colleagues and students at the Eastman School of Music, to Robert Freeman, director of the School, and to his administrative staff, for supporting the publication of the orchestral parts of this edition through a project of ideal instructional scope. During the academic year 1981-1982 a research seminar, devoted to *Messiah* performance problems and including a visit of Professor Jens Peter Larsen of the University of Copenhagen, was linked to a performance of the work, by the Eastman Chorale and the Eastman Symphony Orchestra under the direction of Donald Neuen, in which the students played from printer's proofs; graduate students helped in the editing process; and the production costs were defrayed with the aid of a grant from the School.

The three volumes of the score were issued in the Rutgers University Documents of Music, and their preparation was supported by the John Simon Guggenheim Foundation, the Rutgers University Research Council, and the American Council of Learned Societies. Special mention must be made of the kind help received from my friends Vittorio Versé, Erwin Bodky, Albert Fuller, William Reese, Mogens Wöldike, and from Christopher McCormack and Mario Mercado, my graduate assistants at the Eastman School of Music.

A. M.

[1] Such unison doubling is, in fact, indicated occasionally in Handel's autographs, see e.g. the score for *Solomon*.

[2] See the editor's contribution to *Studies in Renaissance and Baroque Music in Honor of Arthur Mendel* ("Bass Problems in *Messiah*"), Kassel and Hackensack, N.J., 1974.

[3] Jens Peter Larsen, *Handel Studies*, edited by Alfred Mann, special issue of the *American Choral Review*, New York 1972.

[4] Cf. Critical Notes for Nos. 2 and 3 and Nos. 30 and 31.

Messiah

an Oratorio

MESSIAH

AN ORATORIO

Part the First

No. 1 SINFONY

G. F. HANDEL
begun Saturday, August 22, 1741

3

4

No. 2 ACCOMPANIED RECITATIVE

Speak ye com - fort - a - bly to Je - ru - sa - lem, speak ye com - fort - a - bly to Je -

tutti piano
senza fag.

B

ru - sa-lem, and cry un - to_ her, that her war - fare, her war - fare is ac - com-plish'd, that her in -

i - qui - ty is par - don'd, that her in - i - qui - ty is par - don'd.

The voice of him that crieth in the wil-der-ness: Pre-

pare ye the way of the Lord, make straight in the des-ert a high-way for our God.

No. 3 ARIA

Andante
senza rip.

VIOLIN I

VIOLIN II

VIOLA

TENOR

BASSO
CONTINUO

con fag.

and the rough pla - ces plain.

No. 4 CHORUS

14

and all flesh____ shall see____ it to - geth - er, and the glo - ry, the glo - ry of the

and all flesh____ shall see____ it to - geth - er, and the glo - ry, the glo - ry of the

mouth of the Lord hath spo - ken it, and the glo - ry, the glo - ry of the

mouth of the Lord hath spo - ken it, and the glo - ry, the glo - ry of the

Lord, and all flesh____ shall see____ it to - geth - er, the mouth of the Lord hath spo - ken it,

Lord, and all flesh____ shall see it to - geth - er, and the glo - ry, the glo - ry of the Lord shall be re -

Lord, and all flesh____ shall see it, shall see it to - geth - er,

Lord, and all flesh____ shall see____ it to - geth - er,

16

hath spo-ken it, for the mouth of the Lord _____ hath spo - ken it.

hath spo-ken it, for the mouth of the Lord _____ hath spo - ken it.

hath spo-ken it, for the mouth of the Lord,_ the mouth of the Lord_ hath spo - ken it.

hath spo-ken it, for the mouth of the Lord,_ the mouth of the Lord_ hath spo - ken it.

No. 5 *ACCOMPANIED RECITATIVE*

VIOLIN I

VIOLIN II

VIOLA

BASS

Thus saith the Lord, the Lord of Hosts: Yet once, a lit-tle

BASSO CONTINUO

while, and I will shake _____ the heav'ns and the earth, the

sire _____ of all na-tions shall come.

B

The Lord, whom ye seek, shall sud-den-ly come to His tem-ple; ev'n the mes-sen-ger of the Co-ve-nant,

whom ye de-light in, be-hold, He shall come, saith the Lord of Hosts.

21

No. 6 ARIA

for He is like _____ a re-fi - - - - - - -

_E_

- - - ner's _____ fire, _____ who shall stand when He ap -

pear - eth? For He is like _____ a re-fi - - - -

piano f. p. f. p.

piano f. p. f. p.

p. f. p. f. p.

un poco piano

who shall stand when He ap - pear - eth?

For He is like_____ a re - fi - - ner's_ fire,_____ and

who shall stand when He, He ap - pear - eth, when

7 *CHORUS*

And He shall pu - ri - fy, and He shall pu - ri - fy _____ the sons ____ of Le - vi,

And He shall

33

No. 8 RECITATIVE

No. 9 ARIA and CHORUS

attacca Chorus

40

Lord, the glo - ry of the Lord is ris - en up - on thee.

Lord, the glo - ry of the Lord is ris - en up - on thee.

Lord, the glo - ry of the Lord is ris - en up - on thee.

Lord, the glo - ry of the Lord is ris - en up - on thee.

L VLNS. I, II

No. 10 ACCOMPANIED RECITATIVE

up - on thee, and His glo - - - ry shall be seen up - on thee, and His

glo - - ry shall be seen up - on thee. And the Gen-tiles shall come to thy light, and kings to the bright-ness of thy ri - sing.

No. 11 ARIA

Larghetto

senza rip. in octaves with basso cont.

VIOLINS and VIOLA

BASS

The peo - ple that walk-ed in

BASSO CONTINUO

piano

(mf)

con fag.

dwell__ in the land__ of the shad - - ow of death, up - on__ them__ hath the light_____

forte

shi - ned, up - on__ them.hath the light shi - ned.

forte

No. 12 CHORUS

The Might-y God, The Ev - er - last - ing Fa-ther, The Prince of Peace, The Ev - er - last - ing Fa-ther, The

The Might-y God, The Ev - er - last - ing Fa-ther, The Prince of Peace, The Ev - er - last - ing Fa-ther, The

The Might-y God, The Ev - er - last - ing Fa-ther, The Prince of Peace, The Ev - er - last - ing Fa-ther, The

The Might-y God, The Ev - er - last - ing Fa-ther, The Prince of Peace, The Ev - er - last - ing Fa-ther, The

Prince of Peace!

Prince of Peace!

Prince of Peace!

Prince of Peace!

No. 13 PIFA

No. 14 RECITATIVE

There were shep-herds a - bid-ing in the field, keep-ing watch o - ver their flock by night.

ACCOMPANIED RECITATIVE

And lo, the an - gel of the Lord came up - on them,

and the glo - ry of the Lord shone round a - bout them, and they were sore a - fraid.

No. 15 RECITATIVE

And the an - gel said un - to them: Fear not; for be - hold, I bring you good

60

ti - dings of great joy, which shall be to all peo - ple. For un - to you is born this

day, in the ci - ty of Da - vid, a Sa - viour, which is Christ the Lord.

No. 16 ACCOMPANIED RECITATIVE

Allegro
senza rip.

VIOLIN I

VIOLIN II

VIOLA

doubles violoncello

SOPRANO

And sud - den - ly there was with the

BASSO
CONTINUO

(mf)

senza fag.

p

an - gel a mul - ti - tude of the heav'n-ly host, prais-ing God, and say - ing:

61

No. 17 CHORUS

65

No. 18 ARIA

No. 19 RECITATIVE

ALTO

Then shall the eyes of the blind be o-pen'd, and the ears of the deaf un-stop-ped; then

shall the lame man leap as an hart, and the tongue of the dumb shall sing.

No. 20 ARIA

Larghetto e piano
(senza rip.)

He shall feed His flock like a

shep - herd, and He shall ga - ther the lambs with His arm, with His arm, He

come un - to_ Him__ all ye that la - bour, come un - to Him that are_ hea - vy la - den,_ and

He_ will give you rest. Take His yoke up-on you, and learn of Him, for He_ is_ meek_ and

low-ly of heart, and ye shall find rest, and ye shall find rest un-to your souls, take His yoke up-on you, and

learn of Him, for He is meek and low-ly of heart, and ye shall find rest, and ye shall find rest un-

forte

forte

forte

to your souls.

to Chorus:

His yoke

is easy

con fag.

No. 21 CHORUS

Friday, August 28, 1741

81

Part the Second

No. 22 CHORUS

No. 23 ARIA

No. 24 CHORUS

No. 25

95

No. 27 ACCOMPANIED RECITATIVE

No. 28 CHORUS

No. 32 ARIA

No. 33 CHORUS

senza rip.

The Lord strong and might-y, the
The Lord strong and might-y, the
The Lord strong and might-y, the

this King of Glo-ry, who is this King of Glo-ry, who is this King of Glo-ry?

this King of Glo-ry, who is this King of Glo-ry, who is this King of Glo-ry?

B
(con rip.)

Lord strong and might-y, the Lord might-y in bat-tle.

Lord strong and might-y, the Lord might-y in bat-tle.

Lord strong and might-y, the Lord might-y in bat-tle. Lift up your heads, O ye gates, and be ye lift up, ye

Lift up your heads, O ye gates, and be ye lift up ye

Lift up your heads, O ye gates, and be ye lift up, ye

(strings double voices in octaves)

the Lord of Hosts,   He   is the King of Glo - - - - - ry,

Hosts,   He is the King ——— of Glo - - ry,   of Glo - - - - -

the Lord of Hosts,   He   is the King of Glo - ry, of Glo - - - - ry,   of

the Lord of Hosts,   He   is the King of Glo - ry,   of Glo - - - - -

con fag.   5   6   7   6   7   7   7   6   7   7   7   7   3

E

- - - ry, He is the King of Glo - ry, He is the King of Glo - ry,

- - - ry, He is the King of Glo - ry, He is the King of Glo - ry,

Glo - - - - ry, He is the_King of Glo - ry, He is the_King of Glo - ry,

- - - ry, He is the_King of Glo - ry, He is the_King of Glo - ry,

No. 34 RECITATIVE

TENOR

Un-to which of the an-gels said He at a-ny time: Thou art My Son, this day have I be-got-ten Thee?

BASSO
CONTINUO

No. 35 CHORUS

No. 36 ARIA

129

No. 37 CHORUS

No. 39 CHORUS

137

world, _____ un - to the ends of the world.

words un - to the ends_ of the world, _____ un - to the ends of the world.

and their words un - to the ends_ of the world, un - to the ends of the world.

words un - to the ends of the world, _____ un - to the _ ends, un - to the ends of the world.

No. 40 ARIA

to Chorus:

Let us break

their bonds

asunder

ru - lers take coun-sel to - geth - er   a - gainst the Lord   and His a - noint - ed.

senza fag.

No. 41 CHORUS

Let us break their bonds a - sun - der, let _ us   break,

Let   us   break their   bonds   a - sun - der, let _ us

Let   us break their bonds a - sun - der, let us, let _ us   break   their bonds a - sun - der, let us, let us

Let   us break their bonds a - sun - der, let   us,   let   us

from us.

from us.

from us.

from us.

59

No. 42 RECITATIVE

TENOR

He that dwell-eth in heav-en shall laugh them to scorn, the Lord shall have them in de-ri-sion.

BASSO CONTINUO

No. 43 ARIA

Andante
senza rip.

VIOLINS

TENOR

BASSO CONTINUO

con fag.

No. 44 CHORUS

153

154

157

and Lord of Lords, _____ King of

ev-er, Hal-le-lu-jah, Hal-le-lu-jah, for-ev-er and ev-er, Hal-le-lu-jah, Hal-le-lu-jah,

ev-er, Hal-le-lu-jah, Hal-le-lu-jah, for-ev-er and ev-er, Hal-le-lu-jah, Hal-le-lu-jah,

Kings, _____ and Lord of Lords, _____

for-ev-er and ev-er Hal-le-lu-jah, Hal-le-lu-jah, for-ev-er and ev-er Hal-le-lu-jah, Hal-le-

for-ev-er and ev-er Hal-le-lu-jah, Hal-le-lu-jah, for-ev-er and ev-er Hal-le-lu-jah, Hal-le-

for-ev-er and ev-er Hal-le-lu-jah, Hal-le-lu-jah, for-ev-er and ev-er Hal-le-lu-jah, Hal-le-

Sunday, September 6, 1741

Part the Third

No. 45 *ARIA*

sleep, _____ of them that sleep, the first _____ fruits of ___ them that sleep,

con fag.

for now is Christ ris - en, for now is Christ ris - en from ___ the

senza fag.

dead ___

adagio

forte *(tr)*

the first ___ fruits of _____ them that sleep.

f
con fag.

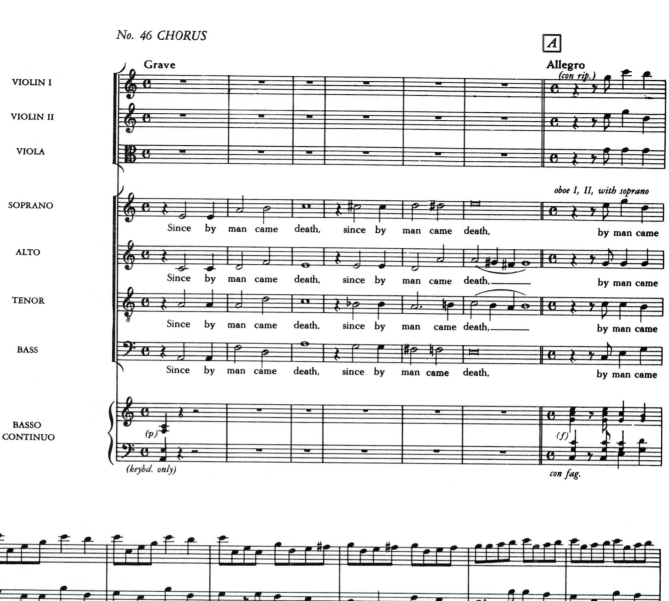

Christ shall all be made a - live, e - ven so in Christ shall all,_____ so in Christ shall all_____ be made a - live, e'en so in

Christ shall all be made a - live, e - ven so in Christ shall all,_____ so in Christ shall all_____ be made a - live, e'en so in

Christ shall all be made a - live, e - ven so in Christ shall all,_____ so in Christ shall all_____ be made a - live, e'en so in

Christ shall all be made a - live, e - ven so in Christ shall all,_____ be made a - live, e'en so in

Christ shall all, shall all be__ made a - live.

Christ shall all, shall all be made a - live.

Christ shall all, shall all be__ made a - live.

Christ shall all, shall all be made a - live.

No. 47 ACCOMPANIED RECITATIVE

Be-hold, I tell you a mys-te-ry; we shall not all sleep, but we shall all be chang'd, in a mo-ment, in the twink-ling of an eye, at the last trum-pet.

No. 48 ARIA

Pomposo, ma non allegro

be rais'd in-cor-rup-ti-ble,   be rais'd in-cor-rup-ti-ble,
_____ in - cor - rup-ti-ble,   in - cor - rup-ti-ble,

89

and   we shall   be chang'd,   be   chang'd,_____

97

176

changd,   and   we shall be— chang'd, _____

and   we   shall be chang'd,   we   shall   be   chang'd, _____

and we shall be chang'd, we shall be chang'd.

187

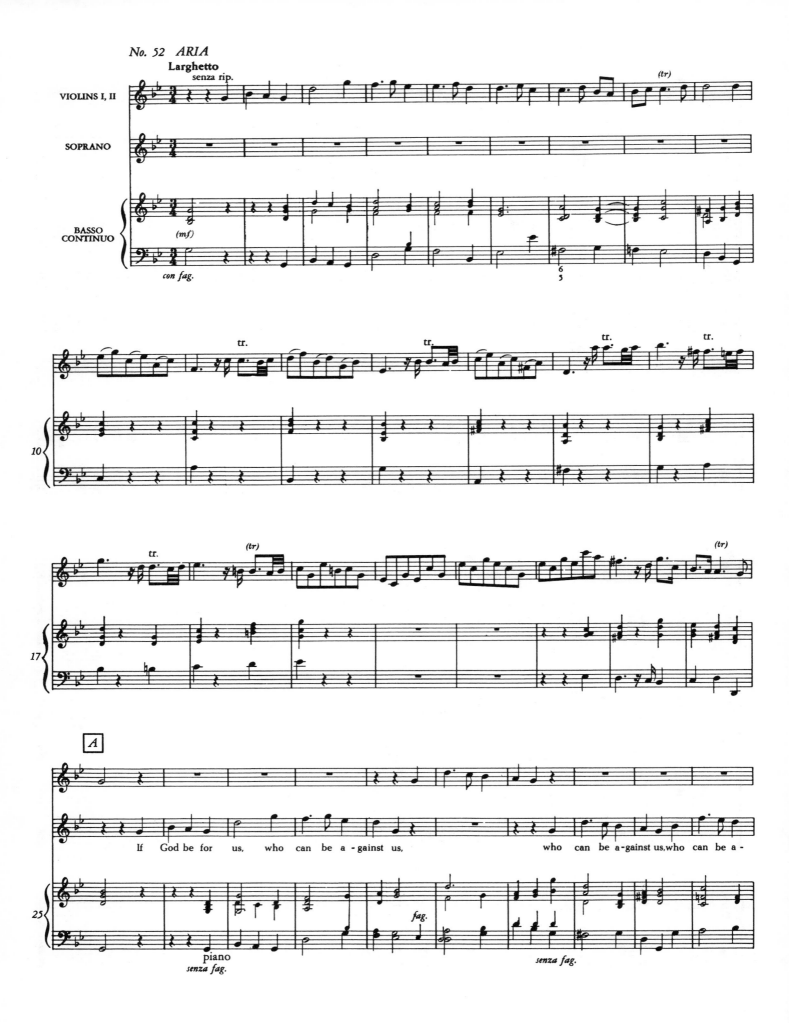

No. 52 ARIA

Larghetto

VIOLINS I, II

SOPRANO

BASSO
CONTINUO

con fag.

If God be for us, who can be a-gainst us, who can be a-gainst us, who can be a-

204

206

208

S.D.G. Fine dell' Oratorio. G. F. Handel.
Saturday, September 12, 1741
orchestration completed Sept. 14

CRITICAL NOTES

CRITICAL NOTES

In order to distinguish between Handel's first Messiah autograph and subsequent additions made by the composer, the word autograph, as used in the following notes, refers only to the volume preserved as the *Original Score* of the work in the British Museum (class mark: R.M.20f.2). The other Messiah manuscripts are identified by their respective locations, while critical commentaries are designated by the names of their authors, as follows:

Tenbury	Handel's conducting score, copied from the autograph by Handel's assistant and copyist, John Christopher Smith, and preserved in the library of St. Michael's College, Tenbury (ms. 346-7).
Hamburg	Conducting score written by Smith for his son, John Christopher Smith the younger, who served as organist in Handel's performances and directed the London Messiah performances after Handel's death; now in the Hamburg State Library (class mark: ND.VI.221).
Coram	A score and complete set of parts, copied from Handel's performance material by several copyists under the direction of J. C. Smith the elder. According to Handel's last will, these copies were presented after his death to the London Foundlings Hospital, now the Thomas Coram Foundation. They are preserved in the Foundation archives.
Fitzwilliam	A collection of Handel autographs preserved in the Fitzwilliam Museum, Cambridge, including sketches for Messiah (class marks: 30H10 and 30H13) which have been reproduced in Chrysander's facsimile edition (see below) and which form part of a group of contrapuntal studies, cf. Alfred Mann, "Eine Kompositionslehre von Händel" in *Händel-Jahrbuch* 1964/65.
Smith Collection	A score from a collection of copies written by J. C. Smith and several other copyists shortly after the Coram copies; now in the British Museum (class mark R. M. 18e. 2).
Randall & Abell	*Messiah, an Oratorio in Score, . . .* London, printed by Messrs. Randall & Abell, [1767], the first complete edition of the work.
Arnold	*The Messiah, an Oratorio . . .* by G. F. Handel, contained in the edition of Handel's works by Samuel Arnold begun in 1786, the first published set of collected works by Handel.
Chrysander	*The Works of G. F. Handel, Part XLV, The Messiah,* edited by Friedrich Chrysander, printed for the German Handel Society, Breitkopf & Härtel, Leipzig, 1902; and Facsimile edition of the autograph, edited for the German Handel Society, Hamburg 1892.
Coopersmith	G. F. Handel, *Messiah, an Oratorio,* edited from the original sources by J. M. Coopersmith, Carl Fischer, Inc., New York, 1946.
Schering	G. F. Händel, *Der Messias,* edited from the autograph score and the parts at the Foundlings Hospital by Arnold Schering and Kurt Soldan, C. F. Peters, Leipzig, 1939.
Spicker	*The Messiah, An Oratorio . . .* by G. F. Handel, edited by T. Tertius Noble, revised according to Handel's Original Score by Max Spicker, G. Schirmer, Inc., New York, 1912.
Steglich	G. F. Händel, *Weihnachtsarie,* Nagels Musik-Archiv no. 104, Kassel, 1953, edited by Rudolf Steglich.
Seiffert	"Die Verzierung der Sologesänge in Händel's Messias" by Max Seiffert, in *Sammelbände der Internationalen Musikgesellschaft,* vol. VIII, pp. 581-615, Leipzig 1907.
Goldschmidt	*Die Lehre von der vokalen Ornamentik,* by Hugo Goldschmidt, Charlottenburg 1907.
Haas	*Aufführungspraxis der Musik,* by Robert Haas, in *Handbuch der Musikgeschichte,* edited by Ernst Bücken, Wildpart-Potsdam, 1931.
Deutsch	*Handel, A Documentary Biography,* by Otto Erich Deutsch, W. W. Norton, New York, 1954.
Larsen	*Handel's Messiah, Origins · Composition · Sources,* by Jens Peter Larsen, W. W. Norton & Co., Inc., New York, 1957.

Myers   *Handel's Messiah, A Touchstone of Taste,* by Robert Manson Myers, New York, 1948.

Prout   *The Messiah, A Sacred Oratorio . . .* by G. F. Handel, edited by Ebenezer Prout, Novello and Co., London, 1902.

Shaw I   "A Handelian Team of 'Messiah' Singers: 1749 or 1750?" by Watkins Shaw, in the *Monthly Musical Record,* vol. 88 no. 989, pp. 169-173, London 1958.

Shaw II   "Covent Garden performances of 'Messiah' in 1749, 1752 and 1753: the evidence of a word-book considered" by Watkins Shaw, in *The Music Review,* vol. XIX, pp. 85-93, London 1958.

In the present edition all dynamic signs and other performance directions which are preserved in Handel's own handwriting appear in Roman type; wherever Handel's wording has been translated, the original text is given in the Critical Notes. The autograph abbreviations p., f., tr., rip. have been so rendered in Roman type. Italic type is used to indicate authoritative source material not preserved in Handel's own handwriting, for instance dynamic signs in the Tenbury and Coram copies.

Roman and Italic type could not be used in strict accordance with this principle in the text for the vocal parts, because Handel omitted the text wherever the intended distribution of words and syllables was easily understood. The complete text has been supplied from the Coram parts. The headings Chorus (or Corus), Recit. (or Rec.), and Accomp. (or Acc.) appear in the Messiah autograph only in Nos. 4, 5 («Accomp.» above the string parts, «Recit.» above the vocal part), 7, 8, 10, 12, 14, 15, 19, 24, 27, 28, 29, 31 («Acc.» above the string parts, «Recit.» above the vocal part), 33, 34, 41, 42, 44, 47, 49, and 51. No. 1 is marked Sinfony, No. 13 is marked Pifa in the autograph. For the present edition, the consistent forms of headings printed in the original word-books for Handel's performances have been adopted; only the heading Song of the original word-books has been changed to Aria or Arioso.

Initial tempo indications are not consistently capitalized in the autograph; adagio (invariably in lower case) is used in the autograph only to indicate a concluding ritenuto.

A listing of instruments and voices at the left margin appears in the autograph only in the instances where particular changes in grouping are concerned (No. 4: V. 1, V. 2, Viol., C, A, T, B; No. 6: originally V. 1 & 2 for the first staff, then changed by Handel to V. 1, with V. 2 and Viol. marked for the second and third staves; No. 9: V. unis.; No. 11: V. unis. e Viola; No. 13: V. 1, V. 2, V. 3, Viola, Bassi; No. 17: T. 1, T. 2; No. 18, first staff: V. unis.; No. 27, the upper three instrument staves: V. 1 & 2, V. 3, Viol.; No. 33, the voice staves: C1, C2, A, T, B; No. 44, the upper three instrument staves: T. 1 & 2, Tymp., V. 1; No. 48: T., V. 1, V. 2, and later V. 2 e Viola for the combined notation of these two parts on one staff; No. 53: T. 1 & 2 at the beginning, T. 1 & 2, Tymp. at measure 72).

Handel's manner of scoring has been reproduced with fidelity. In the autograph only the independent instrumental parts are written out, and doubling parts (other than the basso continuo) are abbreviated or omitted, so that a clear picture of the contrapuntal texture is presented at all times. The notation for the reinforcing parts of oboes I, II and bassoon (*con* and *senza fag.*), given in the present score, outline the oboe and bassoon parts preserved in the Coram set of parts. No oboe or bassoon parts, or reference to such parts, appear in the Messiah autograph except for the independent oboe parts in Chorus No. 39, which was added to the work probably in 1749 (see Larsen, 235f.). Recitative endings in which conclusions of vocal and instrumental parts coincide in the notation of the autograph (Nos. 2, 5, 8, 14, 15, 19, 31, 42, and 49) have been separated in the present edition to conform with prevailing practice. Heavy final bar lines do not appear in the autograph.

The markings by which a small group from the orchestra («senza rip.») was singled out for the accompaniment of arias and some sections of the choruses, appear in the Tenbury copy, beginning with No. 2. They were entered in this copy by Handel (usually above and below the system) probably some time after the first performance. (Handel's indication «con rip. per tutto» has been rendered as «con rip. throughout».)

The use of the treble clef has been substituted in the vocal and basso continuo parts of the present edition for the use of the c-clef in the autograph. The treble clef has been placed in the lower staff of the keyboard part wherever the basso continuo part changes from the bass clef to a higher clef in the sources. Passages written in a higher clef have been transferred to the upper staff of the keyboard part in those cases in which rests are marked for the supporting bass instruments in the Coram parts.

Slurs and staccato marks are indicated as in the autograph and supplemented in a few cases from the other manuscript sources.

Numbers and rehearsal letters used in this edition correspond to those in the editions published by Novello and Co., London, and G. Schirmer, New York.

Editorial additions appear in parentheses. The realization of the basso continuo and suggestions for departures from the original musical text (appoggiaturas; alternative readings in No. 40, bar 19, and No. 48; and alternative notes in the alto part of No. 44, bars 46, 79, see below) appear in small print.

No. 1
Sinfony

The date on which the autograph was begun is entered on the bottom of the first page with the astronomical symbol for the day:

♄ Angefangen den 22 August 1741

The opening Grave has often been presented in double dotted rhythm, see Prout V, Coopersmith VII. Larsen (p. 103) has pointed out that there is not enough justification for accepting this interpretation as the only valid one. The importance of the pattern of even quarters, however, is stressed in the autograph: Handel changed the last two beats in the basso continuo part of bar 8 from

The change was not transferred to some of the secondary copies of the score (See Chrysander X), but it is contained in the Coram parts.

bar 13: Tempo indication in the autograph was originally «andante giusto»; then changed by Handel to «allegro moderato».

The pages containing bars 37-97 of the Sinfony and bars 1-13 of the following recitative are missing in the autograph. In Tenbury, the opening pages, containing bars 1-55 of the Sinfony are missing.

bar 36, viola: In the autograph the first note is written so that it both fills the third space and extends above the fourth line. Coram gives *e,* which is adopted in Chrysander. Randall & Abell gives *d,* which more likely was intended for the entrance accompanying the tonal answer in the bass.

No. 2
Acc Recit.: Comfort ye

bar 3, violin I: Schering points out that the *tr* does not appear in the Coram parts. It is entered, however, in Tenbury.

bar 8: «Ad libitum», entered by Smith in Tenbury (the autograph of this portion has not survived, see above, No. 1), is apparently the only suggestion of a cadenza which has come down to us from the sources used for Handel's own performances, cf. Seiffert 585, Goldschmidt 233f.

bar 15, basso continuo: Tenbury and later copies differ in the second half of the bar from the autograph as follows:

Chrysander mentions that the last two eighth notes could possibly be read as *a* but adopts the version given in the copies, as does Coopersmith. Schering has rightly pointed out that the version

is clear beyond doubt in the autograph.

bar 22, vocal part: Chrysander, Schering and Spicker state that the autograph reads *f♯* but adopt *d♯* from the later sources. Actually, the autograph reads *d♯* (an ink-

spot above the note has doubtless been wrongly interpreted as a correction; the note *d♯,* however, is not crossed out in the autograph).

No. 3
Aria: Every valley

The sources show a considerable number of changes. The autograph and Tenbury originally contained the following additional bar between bars 5 and 6

and the following additional bar between

bars 7 and 8.   Corresponding additions appeared between bars 80 and 81 and between bars 82 and 83. (The last eight bars are not written out in the autograph but indicated after bar 76 with the words. «il Ritornello da capo si scriva fin al segno ⌒». The fermatas which Handel placed on the third beat of bar 9, in order to indicate the end of the portion to be copied, are omitted in the present edition.)

The additional bars were crossed out in pencil in the autograph and pasted over in Tenbury. Similarly, the second half of bar 70 and the first half of bar 71 were crossed out in the autograph. This particular change, however, was apparently later rejected by Handel: In Coram the ritornello appears abbreviated, as indicated in the autograph and Tenbury, but bars 70-71 are left intact.

bar 42, violin I: Appeared in the autograph originally thus:

but was apparently changed to the present form even before Handel filled in the second violin part for this bar (which shows no change).

At the end of the long coloratura on the word "exalted", bar 24, Handel changed the second violin part from

The vocal part in bars 27-28 was changed from

214

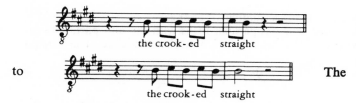

the crook-ed straight

to

the crook-ed straight

The

meaning of the text should be equally observed in bar 73:
an embellishment of the fermata tone would be in conflict
with Handel's treatment of the word "plain". The cadenza,
entered in pencil on a separate line in Tenbury, is by a
considerably later hand (ca. 1790, cf. Seiffert 607 f., Haas
192 ff.). Coopersmith's assumption that this cadenza
appears in the handwriting of Smith (p. IV) is erroneous,
and his suggestion that Handel indicated where it was to
be placed (p. VII) is misleading.

The text in bar 35 of the autograph "straight, and rough
places" was changed by Handel in Tenbury to "straight,
& the rough places". Schering calls attention to the autograph trills in bars 45 and 63 which are omitted in Chrysander (also in Coopersmith). The trills in bars 6 appear
in Coram, but have not been adopted in any of the printed
versions.

bars 71 and 76: Tenbury shows in both instances
Handel's marking «con rip.». This suggests that either bars
73-75 or bars 74-75 were intended to be played senza
ripieno. Rhythmically flexible passages and other intricate
tasks of accompaniment are as a rule assigned to the reduced orchestral group by Handel's notations in the Tenbury copy.

No. 4

Chorus: And the glory of the Lord shall be revealed

vocal parts: Slurs marking the text elisions have been
added in the present edition. Choral entrances are marked
here and in numbers 7, 9, 12, 21, 28 of the autograph with
the indication «tutti».

bar 14: The tutti marking for the instrumental bass is
of particular interest because it is the only indication in
the autograph which suggests Handel's later ripieno markings in Tenbury.

bar 54, basso continuo: The autograph reads

Tenbury and Coram read

bar 91: The entrance in violin II doubling the alto part
was originally written an octave higher in the autograph,
then changed to the present version — a suggestion of the
considerable caution that Handel wished to use in increas-
ing the general dynamic level of this chorus.

bar 119, tenor: The second and third quarters originally
b and *e,* then both changed to *g♯* in the autograph, cf.
Chrysander X.

bars 130-134, oboes: The ties given in Schering appear
only in the first of the oboe parts in the Coram set.

No. 5

Acc. Recit.: Thus saith the Lord

The autograph and Tenbury contained originally a different opening (crossed out in the autograph and pasted
over in Tenbury) in which the beginning of the text was
set as an arioso:

Thus saith the Lord, the Lord of Hosts

It was preceded by an instrumental introduction of three
measures (now recognizable only in outline) which presented this opening theme of the vocal part in imitative
entrances on a pedal point. The original tempo marking
was «Grave». In changing the opening, Handel replaced
the word Grave with «a tempo ordinario». This, in turn,
was replaced through the final change: Handel crossed
out the indication «Recit.» in bar 4 (bar 6 of the original
version) and transferred it to the beginning of the vocal
part, marking the opening of the instrumental parts:
«accomp.» (the same juxtaposition of the two terms occurs in no. 31). In copying the changed version, Smith

retained ⟨notation⟩ for bar 3 of the

basso continuo part in Tenbury and Hamburg (cf. Chrysander X). The original version is of particular interest
because it stresses Handel's interpretation of the text from
Haggai as expressing majesty and compassion rather than
anger. The original entrance of the vocal part bears Handel's dynamic mark *p* for the orchestra. The indication
forte does not appear in the autograph until bar 22.

bars 1 ff.: ⟨notation⟩

should be performed in each instance as ⟨notation⟩
(see bar 3), in the manner of the French overture. A
characteristic of the French string technique is suggested
also in the rhythmic pattern of bars 10-13 (repeated down-
bows; the same pattern appears in no. 7, bars 35-37, and
no. 39, bars 1-4).

No. 6

Aria: But who may abide the day of His coming

The original version of this aria, written for bass and
entirely in 3/8, is contained in the autograph and Tenbury.
It was temporarily replaced by a recitative (Arnold 219).
Handel's manuscript of the present version, which repre-
sents a definitive revision (see Larsen 218, 255), was
written on a separate sheet, probably in 1750 (see Shaw
I, 172 ff.) and later inserted at the end of the original
version in the Tenbury copy. It bears no «senza rip.»
marking, probably because it was not added to Tenbury

until some time after Handel had entered the ripieno markings in this copy.

The indications *con fag.* and *senza fag.* have been supplied from the transposed version of this aria (A minor, for soprano — not, as stated in Schering, for bass) which is the only one contained in Coram.

bar 72, vocal part: Both versions appear in Handel's manuscript (the upper one written slightly smaller).

bar 111, vocal part: Originally  ;

then changed by Handel to the present form.

No. 7

Chorus: And He shall purify

bar 10, alto: Tenbury and Coram read

 ,

the autograph as given here. Chrysander adopted the version of the copies.

bars 15, 16: The entrances of the ripieno group were marked by Handel in Tenbury. The small orchestral group (senza rip.) is to observe the original rests and play the lower tones in the basso continuo part, which represent the version in the autograph (where no ripieno markings are entered) and were thus copied into Tenbury by Smith.

bar 23, tenor: Chrsyander's reading

 , to

which Coopersmith has called attention, is not supported by the sources.

bar 24, soprano: The rhythmic pattern originally followed that of the other parts

and was changed to the present version which lends special emphasis to the word "righteousness".

bar 27, alto: The autograph version

 was

copied into Tenbury and there subsequently changed to

(The change was not made by Chrysander, as suggested in Schering.)

bar 30: The vocal and instrumental bass parts appeared in the autograph originally thus:

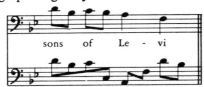

Handel made a number of changes in order to avoid parallel fifths with the alto part. The revision of the vocal bass is not clearly legible. The version

given in the secondary sources and adopted by Chrysander and Schering, is very likely a misreading. Handel did not cross out the upper $b\flat$ but added a separate flag to the note.

bars 36, 37, string parts: cf. No. 5, bars 10-13.

bar 40, alto: Coopersmith states that the first note could be interpreted as either *c* or *d* in the autograph and that the correct reading, corroborated by the preceding alto entrance, is *d*. This reading is not supported by the sources (the autograph and copies show clearly *c*), and it is based on a false premise: melodic variants, even beyond those customarily admitted in the tonal answer, occur frequently in Handel's thematic statements (cf. bars 26, 32, 36 and the entrances in the following chorus No. 9, bars 106 ff.), but Handel is consistent in avoiding unprepared or unresolved $^6_4$ or $^4_3$ positions.

bar 41, viola: Schering changed the viola part to

Very likely the tone *d* on the third beat, effecting a complete chord in the string accompaniment, and the skip into the thematic phrase were fully intended (cf. bar 27, bass).

No. 8

Recitative: Behold, a virgin shall conceive

Handel's spelling in the autograph, "Emanuel", was copied by Smith into Tenbury but there corrected in Handel's handwriting.

bar 6, basso continuo: The ♯ is given in Tenbury.

No. 9

Aria and Chorus: O thou that tellest good tidings to Zion

bars 27, 28, basso continuo: Handel crossed out the ties in the autograph; in the secondary sources they are restored.

bar 105: The autograph bears the notation «attacca il Coro».

bar 133, soprano, tenor, bass parts: Coopersmith states

that 𝅗𝅥 𝅗𝅥 , is correct, not 𝅗𝅥. .

Yet the autograph reads clearly 𝅗𝅥. 𝅗𝅥. in all

three parts.

The autograph ends after bar 139 with the note: «il Ritornello da capo si scriva». The fermatas which Handel placed as indications for the ending (bar 12, on the quarter note *d* of the basso continuo part and on the upper eighth note *d* of the violin part) are omitted in the present edition. In the autograph the continuation is marked only for the violin and basso continuo parts

and in Tenbury, where the last twelve bars are written out, rests are placed in the viola part. Thus no doubling in the viola part (as suggested in Chrysander and Schering) was intended.

No. 10
Acc. Recit.: For behold, darkness shall cover the earth

bar 5, violins: Schering has pointed out that the dotted rhythm on the second eighth note, as given in Chrysander, is not supported by the autograph or secondary sources.

bar 13, viola: The third quarter originally

then changed in the autograph to . Coram reads

No. 11
Aria: The people that walked in darkness

The notation in the upper part (V. unis. e Viola) is discontinued in the autograph after the first note with the indication «all' ottava col Basso». Certain portions are written out again, as indicated here (except for bars 41-43, 50-52, 55-58 and the first half of bar 59, in which the autograph gives the vocal part only). No further direction for the viola part is given in the autograph. In Coram, the viola part doubles alternately the violin and basso continuo parts, as indicated in this edition. Schering differs from Coram, presenting the viola part throughout in unison with the violins. Randall & Abell gives "e Viola" with the basso continuo part.

Coopersmith asserts that there is no justification for leaving large portions of the basso continuo unrealized since Handel did not mark them tasto solo. The autograph, however, specifies this nature of the accompaniment through the indication «all' ottava col Basso».* Actually, a varying texture of the accompaniment is determined through the departures of the basso continuo from the voice and string parts, expressing the meaning of the text with Handelian mastery: the groping unison accompaniment changes to harmony on the word "light", whereas it is completely arrested on the word "death".

---

*Cf. C. P. E. Bach, *On the True Art of Playing Keyboard Instruments*, tr. by W. J. Mitchell, New York 1949, p. 314: "When all performers play in unison it is only natural that the accompanist too should follow the unisons and give up his chords"; see also the full discussion of the basso continuo realization for this aria in Larsen 118-121.

bar 8: Both versions of the vocal part appear in the autograph (the upper notes are written slightly smaller).

On the last note the upper instrumental part of the autograph was originally marked forte, but the notation was subsequently crossed out.

bar 63: Schering points out that a final fermata (given in Chrysander) does not appear in the autograph or Coram.

No. 12
Chorus: For unto us a Child is born

Tempo indication in the autograph originally «allegro». Handel added the word andante at the left margin and then entered the complete tempo indication again below the basso continuo part.

Handel's ripieno marking does not occur in the beginning (as given in Schering) but in bar 3. It is placed above the first violin part and below the basso continuo part (for the basso continuo part clearly on the second eighth note, above violin I at the beginning of the bar).

bar 7, basso continuo: The quarter note and rest indicating the end of the ripieno part were added by Handel in Tenbury.

bar 82, alto: Coopersmith states that a is the correct first note. In the autograph both a and $f\sharp$ are entered but a is crossed out.

No. 13
Pifa

The title suggests shepherds' music played traditionally at Christmas by the Italian pifferari (pipers, shepherds), cf. Myers 74, Larsen 128.

The separate notation for violin III and viola is discontinued in the autograph with the indications «all' ottava col V. 1», «all' ottava col V. 2». The grouping of violins I, II, III occurs again in No. 27. In the Coram set of parts no violin III part is included.

The autograph ends with the eleventh bar (in the middle of a line; the line is completed with the following four bars of recitative). The head of the final dotted half note in the basso continuo part was later filled in by Handel and an eighth note d placed above the dot, followed by a quarter note e and an eighth note $f\sharp$. The three added notes, however, run into the following recitative and are so crowded that they can be read only with difficulty. Therefore Handel was compelled to repeat the entire passage, which due to the lack of space he did above the staff in the letter notation of the old German organ tablature, adding a small loop to the letter f, which indicates sharping according to the tablature symbols. Above the final note of the upper part, Handel entered an N.B. (later crossed out in pencil) referring to an insert, added to the autograph on a half leaf, on which the familiar middle section (ten additional bars) is written, followed by the indication «Da capo». (The fermatas which Handel placed in bar 11 as indications for the ending are omitted in the present edition. An alternate version of the middle section appears on the reverse side of the inserted half leaf but is crossed out.)

The Tenbury copy gives the longer version, including the middle section, but the entire addition, beginning with the bass passage in bar 10 was subsequently crossed out. The last note of bar 10, f, appears without sharp in Smith's handwriting, doubtless because Smith was not familiar with organ tablature. Handel's reversion to the original shorter form of this orchestral interlude is interestingly confirmed by the fact that he did not restore the sharp — obviously essential to the plan of the longer version — in Tenbury (other errors are scrupulously corrected in Handel's handwriting, cf. Nos. 8, 21). Coram and Hamburg contain only the original version. *

No. 14 and No. 15
Recitative: There were shepherds abiding in the field

The accompanied recitative is followed in the autograph by an extended alternate setting of the same text (only the beginning is changed from "and lo" to "but lo"), see Steglich, Chrysander 80 f., Coopersmith 202. This version, written on an inserted sheet, was probably used in performances in 1743 and 1745, but subsequently Handel returned to the original version, see Larsen 219 f. Whereas the autograph contains the original version and the alternate setting, Tenbury contains the original version only.

bars 1 and 10, vocal part: Handel placed three eighth notes above the words "there were" (bar 1) and "they were" (bar 10). The same distribution is still found in Coram (the recitative is omitted in the solo soprano part of the Coram set, but the vocal line is given in the violoncello parts). In the alternate version, however, the words "they were" are repeatedly set as two eighth notes.

No. 16
Acc. Recit.: And suddenly there was with the angel

bar 1: The separate notation of the viola part is discontinued in the autograph with the indication «ut violonc.».

No. 17
Chorus: Glory to God

Between the indications T. 1, T. 2, marking the first appearance of the trumpet parts in the autograph, Handel entered the words «in disparte» (aside), then crossed them out and replaced them with «da lontano e un poco piano». Spicker's assumption (p. V) that the latter indicates a gradual crescendo leading to a choral fortissimo is based on a mistranslation ("as" from a distance) and on a misunderstanding of Handel's use of dynamics: Only the instrumental parts are supplied with dynamic markings in the autograph; the interpretation of the vocal part was determined by the text. Thus Handel's notation refers to the trumpets only, indicating that they are to be placed at a distance (off stage) in the First Part of the work. The intention of actual spatial separation — characteristic of Baroque performance practice — is underlined by the original entry "aside" which Handel evidently wished to intensify through the correction.

bar 19, basso continuo: The autograph reads $\frac{6}{4}$ for the last quarter ($\frac{5}{3}$ as given in Schering is an error).

bar 18: Schering has added a doubling of the vocal bass entrance in the bassoon part. In the two bassoon parts of the Coram set rests are marked for bars 17-20. Contrary to Schering's assumption, these parts do not provide a consistent doubling for the vocal bass.

*See also William H. Cummings, "The Messiah", *The Musical Times*, Vol. 44, 1903, pp. 16-18, and commentary by W. B., p. 184: "The F Sharp in Handel's Pastoral Symphony ('Messiah')".

No. 18
Aria: Rejoice greatly, O daughter of Zion

The original, considerably longer form of this aria, contained in the autograph, shows Handel's notation in two different time signatures. The basso continuo part is written in 4/4, whereas the violin part (marked «unis.») and the vocal part, both containing triplet patterns throughout, are marked 12/8. Reduction to the present length of the aria was indicated by Handel in the autograph. The final version, written on a separate sheet probably in 1749 (see Larsen 220 f.), and later bound into the Tenbury copy, presents the reduced form with changes of all triplet groups to rhythmic patterns in duple meter, so that the entire score appears in 4/4 as given here. Only the upper two parts of the final version show Handel's own handwriting. Handel had the score prepared by letting a copyist (in this case not Smith, see Larsen 220) enter the existing basso continuo part, as well as clefs and signatures for the violin and vocal parts. This procedure, obviously a feasible expedient, since the basso continuo part originally written in 4/4 needed no revision, suggests the haste of performance preparation, and it should be borne in mind that an even more extensive reconciliation of rhythmic patterns may have been intended than is expressed in the dual source. In some cases (bars 5, 33, 40, 41, 75, 104) [♩ ♪ ♪], taken over from the original basso continuo part, should very likely be adapted to [♩ ♪ ♪] of the final version, just as in the original version it was very likely adapted to [♩ ♪] according to the convention of the time (see Larsen 132, 133). The pattern [♪ ♪ ♪] should probably be performed as [♪ ♪ ♪] in bars 42, 43, 106, 107 of the basso continuo part. The two even eighth notes in bar 90 are so written in the autograph. The discrepancy between bars 8 and 107 appears so in Handel's handwriting. The corresponding passage in bar 43 appears in dotted rhythm in the Coram parts. (Schering has pointed out rhythmically inaccurate readings of bars 8, 13, 35 in Chrysander.)

Separate notation for the two violin parts begins in Handel's manuscript with bar 49 and breaks off in bar 58 (in both cases the beginning of a new line).

In the autograph 12/8 version, the bars corresponding to bars 63 and 99 of the final version are marked «adagio».

No. 19
Recitative: Then shall the eyes of the blind be opened
No. 20
Aria: He shall feed His flock like a shepherd

The recitative as well as the entire aria were originally written for soprano. In the autograph, the recitative and bars 1-25 of the aria appear a fourth higher in all parts (except for the basso continuo part, written a fifth lower in the opening of the recitative including the first half of bar 5; other octave transpositions in the basso continuo part occur in bars 9 and 15 of the aria). The original version appears also in Tenbury, but the alto transposition of the recitative and the first half of the aria, as given here, was added to the Tenbury copy, apparently in 1749 (see Shaw II) on a page inserted in front of the original versions of Nos. 19 and 20. The insert ends with bar 25 of the aria, and the continuation is indicated by marking the name of the soprano soloist "Frasi" (Smith's handwriting) at the end of the insert and through a large arrow pointing to bar 26 in the original version of the aria.

Coram gives the original version only (the indications *con fag.* and *senza fag.* are therefore taken from a bassoon part which for bars 1-25 of the aria appears a fourth higher in the manuscript). The conflict of the Coram and Tenbury copies can not be taken as an indication of a reversion to the original form in Handel's performance practice. The divided form of the aria for alto and soprano appears in the Hamburg copy and in several other manuscript copies representing the performance tradition of Handel's last years, see Larsen 225. Nor is the original form consistently presented in Coram: the viola parts of the Coram set show the divided version.

No ripieno marking is given either for the original version or the insert. The marking senza rip. for No. 18 may have been understood to extend through Nos. 19 & 20.

The separate notation of violin I is discontinued in bars 26 and 34 of the autograph with the indication «colla parte». It is intermittently resumed as indicated.

bars 21-22: In the autograph the word "those" is omitted and in both instances lines are placed after the word "lead" indicating that the word was intended to be interpreted through an extended melisma.

The basso continuo figures in bars 12, 16 and 33 have been supplied from the original version.

In the autograph the conclusion of the aria is followed by Handel's notation «segue il Coro His yoke is ease» *(sic)*; the spelling "ease" for easy used throughout No. 21 in the autograph was copied by Smith into Tenbury but there corrected in each instance by Handel.

No. 21
Chorus: His yoke is easy
bar 9, bass: The third quarter reads

in the autograph, cf. note for bars 25, 26, 32.

bar 11: The separate stems and rests indicating the conclusion of the ripieno phrase were entered by Handel in Tenbury.

bars 14-15, viola: The separate entrance of the ripieno part was entered by Handel in Tenbury.

bars 25, 26, 32: The dotted rhythm is not marked in the autograph, but it does appear as indicated in bars 24 and 25 of the alto part and in bar 32 of the soprano part. Tenbury and Coram follow the autograph. In bar 25 Chrysander changed the rhythmic pattern on the first quarter, Schering changed it on the first and third quarters. Cooper-

smith mentions that the dotted rhythm is not marked in bar 26 and supplied it (without mention) in bar 25. The change seems justified in all instances, for with the exception of bar 9 (see above) Handel is consistent in distinguishing the combination of melodic and rhythmic patterns for  and

In fact, on the third quarter of bar 42 the soprano, tenor and bass parts read originally in the autograph and Tenbury, and in both manuscripts the second note of each group was changed a third down and the even rhythm was changed to dotted rhythm.

bar 30, basso continuo: No ripieno marking appears in this bar, but the marking «con rip.» is entered in bars 29 and 34.

bar 31, bass: The autograph reads

In Coram the passage appears changed as given here.

bar 36: Ripieno marking in Tenbury: «con Rip. continuando».

The date for the completion of Part I is entered in the autograph with the astronomical symbol for the day: August 28 ♀ 1741.

No. 22
Chorus: Behold the Lamb of God
The autograph contains a number of changes in the opening bars. The beginning was apparently written down at first as follows:

and then changed to the present form. The original rhythmic pattern (retained in the viola entrance and recurring in bars 7-8, 13-14) suggests a basic tempo in four rather than eight beats. The eighth notes are doubtless meant to be given their full rhythmic value (see upbeats to bars 3, 6, 7).

bar 8, alto: The present version, anticipating and stressing the words of the following bar, appears in the autograph and all other sources from Handel's time. The reading

which is adopted in Chrysander, Schering, and Coopersmith, appears first in the Hamburg copy (written probably after Handel's death).

No. 23
Aria: He was despised

bars 18-33: Missing in Tenbury (two pages).

bar 40, vlns. I and II: In the autograph, no ties are marked from this to the following bar. In Tenbury and Coram, ties have been added, but they are not consistently marked: the upper part only is tied in Tenbury (Smith's writing), and the Coram parts follow Tenbury.

bar. 66, vocal part: The dotted rhythm on the last quarter appears in the autograph. Tenbury, Coram, and Hamburg present the two notes in even rhythm. Chrysander mentions both versions but adopts that of the copies.

No. 24
Chorus: Surely He hath borne our griefs

bars 1 ff: 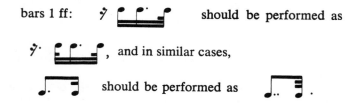 should be performed as

, and in similar cases,

should be performed as

.

(see combination of rhythmic patterns, bars 2, 3, 6ff.).

bar 13, vla: Chrysander changed the first two notes, as follows:

because he assumed that the unison doubling with vln. II was due to an oversight by Handel. Schering rejected this change because of hidden fifths with the bass, but added a tie from bar 12 to bar 13. The use of brief unison passages underlining important melodic contours is a characteristic device of Handel's part writing (see No. 35, bar 2; No. 37, bar 7).

No. 25
Chorus: And with His stripes we are healed

bar 1, basso cont: The first note appears in the autograph and all copies of the score but not in the Coram parts. Apparently the first keyboard chord was not to be supported by other instruments (Schering's edition differs in this point from Coram).

bars 4 ff: In the autograph, the two words "we are" (spelt "wee are") appear only in this, not in reversed order. Tenbury has "are we" (Smith's writing). Cf. Coopersmith, IX; Chrysander's and Schering's notes concerning this point are not accurate.

bar 4, vln. I, sopr. and basso cont: Originally

Handel changed the violin I and soprano parts in the autograph.

bars 8 and 13, string parts: The separate notation of the doubling string parts is broken off in the autograph with the following indications: ut C. (Cantus), ut Alt, ut Tenor. Only one variant from the vocal part is written out for vln. II (bars 62-72). In Tenbury, the separate notation of the string parts is continued beyond these points and additional stems and (for vln. I and vla.) notes are entered in Handel's handwriting to mark the entrance of the ripieno group in bar 19. The whole note in vln. I, bar 19, is written by Smith, the half rest and half note by Handel. The vla. notes in bars 20-21 are written by Handel, the rests in the same bars by Smith. The whole note in bar 19 and the rests in bars 20-21 refer to the small string group (senza rip).

bar 71, alto: The two tones given for the second quarter appear in equal size in the autograph. As the violin part shows, the upper tone is to be preferred. (The lower tone was meant for the men's voices in the alto section. The support of men's voices should still be used for the preceding alto entrance).

No. 26
Chorus: All we like sheep have gone astray

Tempo indication in the autograph: allegro moderato; in Tenbury: a tempo ordinario (Smith's writing).

string parts: For style of bowing see the original slurs in bars 52 ff.

bar 65, alto, the last two tones: See note for No. 25, bar 71.

Nos. 24, 25, 26 are joined in the autograph: the first change of tempo (alla breve moderato) occurs in the middle of a line, the final section (allegro moderato) is linked to the preceding sections by additions of naturals to the new signature (a device not used elsewhere in the autograph). The fugue ended originally with a full F Minor cadence which Handel then shortened to the present half close. Cf. notes on text and key-relationship, Coopersmith IX, Larsen 42 ff. The signature of three flats (Dorian) is used in the autograph for Nos. 24 and 25. D flat is marked by accidental in each instance except No. 25, bar 45, bass and basso continuo parts.

No. 27
Acc. Recit.: All they that see Him laugh Him to Scorn

In the autograph, the vocal part is written in the tenor clef; but according to the names of soloists, which Handel added in the autograph and Tenbury, it was assigned to a soprano rather than tenor in some of his performances (cf. Larsen pp. 226-7).

The grouping of vlns. I, II, III suggests a division of forces, even within the small string group (senza rip.), that favors the presentation of the rhythmic pattern in the upper part — the rhythmic pattern symbolizing the scenes of derision and scourging in the orchestral accompaniment of the Baroque Passion settings.

No. 28
Chorus: He trusted in God that He would deliver Him

The autograph shows two versions of the text: "that He might deliver Him" (bars 2 ff.) and "that He would deliver Him" (bar 58). In Tenbury "might" is changed to "would" in each instance.

bar 8, tenor: Text in the autograph: "If He delight in Him"; text in Tenbury: "Let Him deliver Him".

bar 8, basso cont:

appears as a continuation of the preceding bar in the autograph, but was crossed out by Handel in favor of the present version which suggests that a fuller accompaniment is to begin with this bar.

bar 8, string parts: The notation of the string parts stops in the autograph with the following indications: ut Cant:, ut Alt:, ut Tenor. The variant for vln. I, bars 52-53, is written out. Schering calls attention to the fact that the tenor part is written

whereas the doubling viola part is written

in the autograph, and he applies a similar pattern to bar 12 (alto — vln. II). Doubtless the quarters should be played broadly and disguise the singers' taking a breath. In Tenbury and Coram, however, the difference in notation is not observed throughout, nor is it strictly carried out in Schering.

bar 42, basso cont: 6̄ in autograph (cf. Chrysander XII).

bar 57, basso cont: The last quarter note appears undivided in the autograph, Tenbury, and Coram, but divided in other manuscript sources, cf. Chrysander XII.

No.29
Acc. Recit.: Thy rebuke hath broken His heart
vocal part: cf. No. 27.

bars 2 and 3, tenor: Handel's changes in the autograph give particular emphasis to the halting effect in the declamation of the words "He is full of heaviness". The original melodic line seems to have been

(only the first two tones are clearly legible), then Handel changed the second tone to *f*, the third tone to *a*, and added the following eighth rest.

bar 7, vlns. I and II: Schering (unlike Chrysander) omits the trills, stating that they are not adequately represented in the sources. The trills are not indicated in Tenbury or Coram, but in the autograph the usual abbreviation tr. (t. in vln. II), though faded, appears in Handel's writing.

No. 30
Arioso: Behold, and see if there be any sorrow
vocal part: cf. No. 27.

bar 2, vocal part: The appoggiatura appears in the autograph as follows:

bar 7: The separate notation of vln. II is discontinued in the autograph with the indication: unis.

No. 31
Acc. Recit.: He was cut off out of the land of the living
vocal part: cf. No. 27.

bar 2, vocal part: In the autograph, no appoggiatura to the first tone is marked (the appoggiatura added in Spicker is due to a misreading of the ♯).

No. 32
Aria: But Thou didst not leave His soul in hell
vocal part: cf. No. 27.

No. 33
Chorus: Lift up your heads, O ye gates

In Tenbury, "Boys" is marked in pencil (by a later hand) for sopr. II. Thus sopr. I was allotted to the women soloists. In the autograph the two separate systems for sopr. I and II, marked C (Cantus) 1 and C 2 are reduced to one system marked C 1 & 2.

bar 5, vln. II: Chrysander and Schering, following earlier editions, assumed that the last tone *a* is a mistake in the autograph, and changed it to *c*. Very likely the slight disparity of sopr. II and vln. II was fully intended (*c* to be taken by ob. I. II, vln. I, sopr. I, II; *a* to be taken by vln. II, vla., alto). Tenbury and Coram also give *a*.

bars 5-10, basso cont: Schering points out that these measures were taken over into the Coram parts by mistake since the autograph shows them in alto clef. To Schering's note should be added that in Coram, by a further mistake, the tenor clef is marked in bar 5, giving the following notation:

 etc.

bar 11: In the autograph, the dotted rhythm on the sec-

ond quarter is marked only for the tenor; in Tenbury and Coram it is marked for all parts (the notation in bars 14 and 15 appears as given here in both the autograph and Tenbury).

bars 18-61: The pages on which these bars were written are missing in Tenbury, thus no original ripieno markings have been preserved for bars 19, 26, 29. The last con rip., marked in No. 33, may have been understood to extend throughout No. 35, for which no special ripieno marking is given in the autograph.

bars 43, 47, 49: The notation of the string parts is discontinued in the autograph as indicated.

bar 63: The last note in the alto is *e*, the last note in the tenor is *g* in the autograph and Tenbury.

bar 74, alto: The last note is *f* in the autograph. Tenbury has *a* (Smith's writing).

No. 35
Chorus: Let all the angels of God worship Him
rip. marking, see note for No. 33, bars 18-61.

bars 9, 10: The notation of the string parts is discontinued in the autograph with the following indications: ut C., ut A, ut T.

bar 10, alto, and bar 15, tenor: The two notes on the third quarter are written in equal size in the autograph (cf. note for No. 25, bar 71).

bar 22, alto: The changed distribution of the text in Tenbury

God wor - ship, wor -

(adopted in the later sources and in Chrysander and Schering) does not appear in Handel's writing.

No. 36
Aria: Thou art gone up on high
This aria, originally for bass, was rewritten several times for alto. Handel's manuscript of the present version was written on a separate sheet, probably in 1750 (see Shaw I, 171), and later bound into the Tenbury copy. In Chrysander's editorial note, the following reference is made to the beginning of this version in his facsimile edition: "The plate reproduction does not clearly show that Handel crossed out the word 'Allegro', Only the tempo indication 'Larghetto' retains validity". Chrysander's assumption that the word Allegro was crossed out is probably an error. The word seems faded and blotted rather than crossed out. It appears at the extreme left margin (of a right page) in a very light shade of ink, whereas the word Larghetto is lined up with the beginning of the staves and written in the darker shade of ink used for the entire aria. Thus Allegro was very likely added later and blotted or smeared through page turning before the aria was bound into the Tenbury copy. This point, though small in itself, suggests a sequence of alterations which is important and which might help towards resolving the "prejudices with which traditional assessments have burdened this aria" (Larsen, 157). The first version of the aria, contained in the autograph but probably never performed by Handel, was marked Allegro. Later Handel changed the tempo marking to Andante (version B, probably used 1743-1749) and Larghetto (the present version, probably used until Handel's death; the chronology of the different versions is given in Larsen, 229). In settling this definitive version, however, Handel evidently decided on a marking for the tempo (or rather: character) of the aria that blended the original "lively" with the later "somewhat broad". Handel's marking Allegro larghetto, seemingly a contradiction in terms, underlines the textual dualism of the Ascension Day gospel to which Larsen has called attention (p. 156). But we might well dispute Larsen's assumption that Handel's setting of this text was not guided by a unifying idea. The very opening, the turn from the preceding D Major tutti to the D Minor of the small ensemble, suggests the typically reflective situation of the aria given to the expression of a single "affection". The instrumental passages in eighth and sixteenth notes must represent the marking Allegro larghetto as much as the vocal line: they are to be performed neither in a sprightly manner nor heavily. The basic "affection" they express is not militant but serene.

Handel's manuscript bears no senza rip. marking, since it was probably not added to Tenbury until some time after Handel had entered the ripieno markings in this copy.

The slurs in bar 7 and the markings piano in bar 15 and forte in bar 37 have been supplied from the corresponding measures in version A (autograph), the indications *con fag.* and *senza fag.* have been supplied from the transposed version of this aria (G Minor, version D) which is the only one contained in Coram.

No. 37
Chorus: The Lord gave the word
bar 14, vla: The first two notes appear as even eighth notes in the autograph. The dotted rhythm is marked in Tenbury and later manuscript sources.

No. 38
Aria: How beautiful are the feet of them
The text for this aria and the following chorus is to be understood as one unit. The present form of No. 38 appears in the autograph as first section of a da capo aria and is followed by a setting of "Their sound is gone out" as middle section (with divided violin parts). Handel wrote several new settings for the entire text. The present version, combining the first section of the original aria with the choral setting of "Their sound is gone out", was apparently his final choice, see Larsen, 230 ff. No ripieno marking appears in Tenbury, possibly because this aria was still "A Song omitted in the performance" when Handel entered the ripieno markings, see Larsen, 234.

No. 39
Chorus: Their sound is gone out into all lands

This chorus, probably written in 1749 (see Larsen, 235 f.) was later added to the autograph. The oboe parts appear below the violin and viola parts in the autograph. In Tenbury, the parts are specially marked: V:1, V:2, Viola, H.1, H.2 (Smith's writing).

The first four bars of the string parts show a rhythmic pattern which Handel favored in his orchestral writing throughout his life (see also Chorus No. 7, "And He shall purify", bars 36-37). It suggests a specially pointed use of the French "Rule of the Down Bow" (downbow for every heavy beat) to which Handel's Italian contemporaries were opposed. Handel however, "well acquainted with the nature and management of the violin", had declared himself for the French violinistic style in his famous early encounter with Corelli (see Geminiani's *Art of Playing on the Violin*, facs. ed. by David Boyden, Oxford University Press, 1952, p. V, and Deutsch, 17).

No. 40
Aria: Why do the nations so furiously rage

The original, considerably longer form of this aria, contained in the autograph, is also included in Tenbury (in Smith's writing). After bar 38, however, a pencil line is drawn vertically through the staves, and the following bars of the original version are crossed out. The new ending (bars 39-45) is based on thematic material from the original remainder of the aria, presenting the harmonic scheme in strikingly condensed form but elaborating upon the original vocal and instrumental setting of the E Minor cadence. It is added (in Handel's writing) on a separate sheet and bound as last page into the Tenbury copy. Bar 45, concluded with a single bar line, is followed by Handel's notation: "Coro let us break their Bonds asunder" (suggesting an attacca connection to the following chorus, cf. Larsen 237, Coopersmith X). Larsen, 165, 236 f., 257 f., points out that in several copies written later than Tenbury, the aria appears again in the original form. But Tenbury shows no indication to the effect that Handel rejected the shortened form subsequently, and the shortened form is adopted in those copies which, next to Tenbury, are most closely linked to Handel's performance practice — Coram and Hamburg; the later copies, containing the original form of the aria, did not serve as conducting scores.

bar 5: The separate notation of vln. II is discontinued (in the autograph half-a-measure earlier than here) with the indication: unis. The same indication appears in bar 28.

bar 19, vocal part: The next-to-last eighth note is blotted in the autograph and could be read as either *b* or *a*. Preference might be given to *b*, since conjunct eighth-note motion is favored throughout the original setting of the aria. All later sources, however, give *a*.

bar 42: At the beginning of the bar originally two eighth notes *a* in the vocal part and *c* in the basso continuo, then changed by Handel as given here.

No. 41
Chorus: Let us break their bonds asunder

The ties are inconsistently marked in the continuo part of the autograph (they appear in bars 11-14 and 19-20 but not in bars 36-37 and 39) and in all instrumental parts of the Tenbury copy. Schering has called attention to the fact that the autograph contains ties for the string parts only in bars 11, 63, and 64, that Handel crossed them out in bars 63-64, and that they are not marked in Coram. This account is not fully accurate: in the Coram parts for violins and violas the ties are as inconsistently marked as in the Tenbury copy, but the tie in bar 11 of the autograph, like those in bars 63-64, was marked and subsequently crossed out. Thus there is consistent marking in the string parts of the autograph and in the woodwind and violoncello parts of the Coram set. According to this, the sixteenths were intended to be played separately throughout by violins and violas, whereas the other instrumental parts were probably meant to conform to the vocal parts which they support.

bar 32: Schering points out that only the first quarter appears in the Coram violoncello and bassoon parts and adds a second quarter, as follows:

stating that this appears in the autograph. Actually, the autograph shows the lower *g* as an eighth note which, like the following eighth notes, was apparently intended only for the keyboard continuo but not for the supporting strings and bassoons.

bar 58, vln. I: Schering changed the second note to *f*. The autograph and all other sources have *d*. Very likely the slight disparity between vln. I and sopranos and oboes, effecting a $^6_5$ chord in the last tutti cadence, was fully intended.

No. 43
Aria: Thou shalt break them

In the autograph no slurs are marked in bars 13, 15, 20, 24, 25, 30, 32, 33, 36, 38, 39, 51, 58, 61, 66, 67, 68. In Coram, the marking is somewhat fuller but not entirely consistent.

bar 38, vlns: Tenbury, Coram and Hamburg differ from the autograph in this bar as follows:

Chrysander assumed that the mistake was in the autograph and adopted the versions given in the copies. Schering, pointing out the similarity with bars 11-13, reverted to the autograph version, as does the present edition.

No. 44
Chorus: Hallelujah

bar 1, vln I: In the autograph the beginning was originally written as follows:

and then revised

to the present form. The change underlines both Handel's wish to place the main accent of the theme on the first eighth of the third beat rather than the first beat and his concern with the shape of the entire opening phrase and its unfolding towards the choral entrance. Oboes I, II are marked in the Coram score as supporting violins I, II: V. H. 1; V. H. 2 (oboes I, II appear in separate notation only in the Coram parts, not in the Coram score). The Coram oboe parts for this chorus double the soprano part throughout, not the violin parts. Thus the error in the Coram score applies not only to the introduction, as noted in Chrysander XIII, but to the entire chorus.

bar 21, trpt. II: Fifth eighth note ƒ♯ in the autograph and Tenbury.

bars 23 ff., vocal parts: The text elisions are implied by the note values but are not specifically marked in the autograph (as suggested in Coopersmith, XI), since the repetition of the word "Hallelujah" is not written out but indicated by 𝄌 in the instances concerned.

bar 38, basso cont: The figures given for the last quarter are ⅗ in the autograph (cf. Chrysander, XIII).

bar 46, alto: Only the lower of the two notes is marked in the autograph and Tenbury (cf. No. 25, bar 71).

bar 74, trpts: Indication in the autograph: unis.

bars 76-77, vocal parts: The text is not filled out by Handel. In the autograph, two versions appear in Smith's writing, as given here. The Coram parts follow the autograph.

bar 79, alto: The two notes on the first quarter appear in equal size in the autograph (cf. No. 25, bar 71). The second quarter reads *a* in the autograph and Tenbury. In the similar alto entrance, bar 46, Handel wrote first *a*, then changed it to ƒ♯

bar 91: In this bar only, the autograph shows the spelling "alleluja" (the text is entered for soprano and bass parts).

The date for the completion of Part II is entered in the autograph with the astronomical symbol for the day: an ☉ Septembr 6.

No. 45
Aria: I know that my Redeemer liveth

The autograph contains several changes in the placement of text. In measures 107-108 and 109-110, «shall I» read originally «I shall». Measures 125-129 were originally written as follows:

the   first   fruits   of   them   that   sleep

Similarly, measures 135-137 read originally

fruits   of   them   that   sleep

In re-writing these passages, Handel added the eighth note appoggiatura on the tone *e,* to which the word «that»

is allotted in measure 136, and he made a corresponding change in measure 152, although in this case he indicated no change in the disposition of the text.

The word «liveth» was originally set to a half note in measures 22, 43, and 96, but evidently changed by Handel before the composition of the aria was completed; measure 115 of the autograph shows the notation in quarter notes only.

bar 151: «adagio» is marked on the quarter note rather than on the half note in the Tenbury copy.

No. 46
Chorus: Since by man came death

Schering points out that the first note in measure 1 and the first note in measure 17 indicate keyboard chords without orchestral support, since they are not included in the Coram parts. Actually, the measures of the a cappella phrases are not even marked by rests in the Coram parts; only the words «Since by man came death» and «For as in Adam all die» are inserted before the beginning of the corresponding Allegro sections.

The opening portion of the text, I Corinthians XV: 21, was originally used twice for the Grave-Allegro sequence. Handel subsequently crossed out the repeated text in measures 17-34 of the autograph and replaced it with I Corinthians XV:22. The autograph shows the spelling «death» instead of «dead». The error was copied by Smith into the Tenbury score but corrected there by Handel.

The first four measures of the autograph show considerable changes resulting in an intensification of the entire opening a cappella phrase. The measures appeared originally as follows:

No. 47
Acc. Recit.: Behold, I tell you a mystery

No. 48
Aria: The trumpet shall sound

bar 4, violin I: Handel crossed out [music example] in the autograph and wrote [music example] instead.

The mysterious quality of the setting of I Corinthians XV:51 thus emphasized is nevertheless a quality of dynamic strength. This is the only accompanied recitative in the work in which Handel uses the full string orchestra from the outset. Handel's interpretation of the text is enhanced by two further changes in the autograph: The sixteenths beginning in the fifth measure (and anticipating, as Larsen points out, the pattern of repeated tones in the aria) appear obviously as an afterthought

chang'd in a mo- ment, in the

and in the original tempo marking for the aria, «andante ma non allegro», Handel replaced «andante» with «Pomposo».

The *Da capo* is indicated in the autograph as follows:

- ty Da Capo

In the Tenbury copy Handel changed the vocal part of this measure to

- ty. The

and in Smith's hand is entered «Da capo dal segno 𝄋». The corresponding mark 𝄋 was added by Smith at the beginning of measure 29; the Coram copies show the revised version.

The separate notation of violin I is discontinued after the initial upbeat for the first seven measures with the notation «unis. colla Tromba», and it is again discontinued in measures 141-147. In order to be able to place two systems on each page, Handel used five staves for the six-part score from measure 29 to measure 156, combining the parts of violin II and viola on one staff in the alto clef.

In measures 38, 39, 40, measures 51, 52, 53, measures 91, 92, 93, and measures 94, 95, 96, Handel's original setting of the word «incorruptible» (an unusual error in prosody) appears changed as early as the Smith collection

copy (ca. 1760, cf. Larsen 209). That it remained unaltered in the earlier sources may be due to the fact that the bass part was sung by a German singer, Thomas Reinhold, from the first London performance until his death in 1751 (in distinction to numerous changes of soloists' names which Handel marked in the Tenbury copy for other arias, his annotation for this aria reads «Reinhold stat»).

No. 49
Recitative: Then shall be brought to pass
The signature contains only one flat in the autograph.

No. 50
Duet: O death, where is thy sting

No. 51
Chorus: But thanks be to God
As part of the autograph, the duet appears in a considerably longer form which was also copied into the Tenbury score. In the longer version, the alto part of measure 5 reads

O grave

and it is followed by seventeen measures which were pasted over in the Tenbury copy. The changes necessary to connect measure 5 to measure 6 (originally measure 23) in the Tenbury copy show the handwriting of both Handel and Smith: Handel crossed out the quarter rest at the end of the measure, added an eighth flag to the quarter note e♭, and entered the text; Smith added the last three eighth notes.

bar 12, alto: The autograph reads as follows:

sting? O grave

This version was originally copied into the Tenbury score but subsequently changed to the present version.

The autograph version of the chorus has been subjected to the following two small editorial changes which are not supported by source material and through which the polyphonic texture is touched up in a manner not actually consistent with Handel's principles of part writing:

bar 48, violin II: The last eighth note is changed in Chrysander's and Schering's editions to b♭ in order to avoid parallel octaves with the basso continuo part. The melodic line of the basso continuo, however, serves in this passage briefly as a reinforcement for that of the tenor which is doubled in octaves by the second violin part throughout the phrase;

bar 70, tenor: The second note is changed in Schering's edition to e♭, thus rendering the passage different from all other statements of this theme. The use of repeated tones, establishing brief pedal point effects in various parts against passing dissonances is idiomatic to Handel's contrapuntal style.

bar 61, soprano: The second note is given as c in the autograph and in the Tenbury copy. In this case the correction, adjusting the soprano part to the part of violin I (and to the melodic pattern of both parts in the preceding measure) is corroborated by later manuscript sources including the Coram copies.

bar 31, alto: Coopersmith states that the reading

is incorrect, and that the autograph shows

The autograph version, however, contains no slur, nor is the intended distribution of text unequivocally clear.

No. 52
Aria: If God be for us

The placing of the text, as given in measures 25-27 and 37-39 of the autograph, was copied into the Tenbury score, but here changed by a later hand (involving in the first case the change from «be» to «is»), as follows:

The changes were taken over in the Coram copies. A comparison of the original and changed versions obviously points out arguments of musical consistency and preferences in prosody. The revised version may have been suggested by one of Handel's soloists, possibly the famous Mrs. Cibber, who sang the aria transposed to C Minor in the first performance (see Larsen, 240; the transposition was used again for other alto soloists who sang under Handel's direction, cf. also Shaw I 171 ff.). It is conceivable that the altered text setting was accepted by Handel, but it cannot be considered the "correct" version (as in Chrysander, XIII).

bar 89, vocal part: The placing of the dotted eighth and sixteenth notes appears so in the autograph: the rhythmic pattern is combined with the melodic pattern, not with the metric pattern.

No. 53
Chorus: Worthy is the Lamb

The first tempo marking was changed twice in the autograph. «A tempo ordinario» was entered above «Largo» but subsequently crossed out. «Largo», in turn, appeared originally as «Larghetto». It is likely that these changes were made in deciding the sequence of Largo-Andante, as Larsen suggests, and that these two tempo indications should accordingly be understood as marking no more than slight deviations from a "tempo ordinario".

bar 20, viola: The autograph reads

In the other sources only c♯ is indicated for the third eighth note.

In the autograph and in the Tenbury copy appear notations suggesting that Handel contemplated two shortened versions of the final chorus for performance. In the autograph, Handel drew large vertical pencil strokes before the fourth beat of measure 39 and the fourth beat of measure 53 through the entire score, and he entered, again in pencil, the upbeat entrance of trumpet and kettle drums from measure 53 in measure 39 (for a skip from measure 39 to measure 54). In the Tenbury copy, Handel added «God, for ever and ever Amen, Amen» as alternate text in measures 26-28 and sketched the following bass cadence after measure 71 at the margin:

This change would have meant an even more drastic shortening of the final chorus that the omission of measures 39-53: a conclusion without the Amen fugue (cf. Larsen, 184).

The Amen fugue, for which extensive studies exist among the Fitzwilliam manuscripts in Cambridge, shows a number of revisions in the autograph, the most important of which affect both the beginning and end of the vocal and instrumental bass parts. Measures 74-77 seem to have read originally

Measures 151-155 apparently read

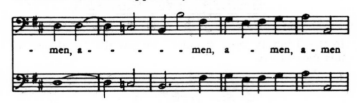

The change at the beginning of the fugue may account for the fact that Handel did not interrupt the melisma in the tenor part of measure 80 (originally ascending diatonically like the bass part in measure 75), as he did in all similar passages. Measures 139-142, in which Handel placed at first the part of violin I in the staff for violin II, contain Smith's correction in the autograph; but there seems no justification for Schering's assumption that the letters «S[oli] D[eo] G[loria]» at the end show a hand other than Handel's.

The completion of the work is dated in the autograph as follows:

S. D. G.

Fine dell' Oratorio   G. F. Handel   ♭ Septembr 12
1741

ausgefüllet den 14. dieses